Crushing Call Reluctance for Loan Officers

A Proven System to Make the Calls You Need to Get the Business You Want

By Carl White and Kevin Gillespie

FREE – Strategy Call

This Book Includes a Free Strategy Call You Can Use RIGHT NOW to Tame Call Reluctance. Get Some of Our Best Scripts on This Call. When You Know What to Say, Call Reluctance is Reduced.

Get It NOW at
CrushingCallReluctance.com/Call

Published by
Mortgage Marketing Animals
Palm Harbor, FL
MortgageMarketingAnimals.com

Names: White, Carl, author. Gillespie, Kevin, author.
Woodard, Sue, foreword.
Title: Crushing Call Reluctance
Description: First edition | Florida: The Marketing Animals, 2018
ISBN-13: 978-1-7324655-0-3 (paperback)
First Edition: August 2018

Limit of Liability/Disclaimer of Warranty

Dedication

We dedicate this book to

The Freedom Club –

the most awesome group of loan

officers on the planet. It's your

inspiration and your stories that

have made this book come to

reality. We are forever grateful.

Foreword

Sam was one of the biggest real estate agents in town, and I'd always wanted to work with him. One fine day, his name came across as the listing agent for a property my clients were buying. Here was my chance! I picked up the phone – then set it back down again – I had to get the words just right. What if he answered? Wait, what if he didn't answer? I felt a bead of sweat on my lip – ick. Maybe I'd just wait and call tomorrow. Or next week, that might be better – I'd have a chance to think about what to say. Or maybe I'd just wait until closing – yeah, that's the ticket …

We've all been there. We know what we need to do – the call we need to make, the person we need to connect with, the conversation that needs to take place – and yet we don't make the move. And, worse, we look back later and know we have foiled ourselves once again by putting the right actions off – and we haven't truly served those who might need to hear exactly what we uniquely have to share. So why do we let this happen - getting stuck in this "knowledge-action" gap?

With more than twenty-five years under my belt in the mortgage industry – as an originator, speaker and executive – I've come face to face with this issue many times, both in myself as well as the many who I've had the honor to train and lead.

For some, it's a war against garden variety procrastination (I personally know this one well – I put the PRO in procrastination!) For others, the right actions get lost in the insidious pursuit of perfection. For still others, they suffer a debilitating fear of rejection or being judged. These are real issues that we all face on some level. But every single successful person I know has sought out and found ways to overcome these issues, usually involving a lot of trial, error and mistakes along the way.

So what if you had a playbook? What if hundreds of years of expertise were distilled into a step-by-step guide? What if you had the tools to finally defeat your call reluctance once and for all? Enter the book you are lucky enough to be holding in your hands right now, crafted by some of the very best minds in the business.

In the mortgage industry, Carl White and Kevin Gillespie are well-known as experts and leaders – but not as many know them on a personal level.

I was honored to work with Kevin "back in the day". He was always known as a strong and respected leader and colleague before, during and after the 2008 crash we lived through together. Even during the most difficult times in our industry, he was a consistent source of strength and guidance – and Kevin now continues to serve and give in an increasingly significant way.

Carl was more of a mystery to me over the years as we crossed paths at various industry events. We never seemed to have time to do more than a quick hello – always leaving me curious about what these wild and wonderful "Mortgage Marketing Animals" were up to, and why they seemed to have such a ridiculously devoted following amongst so many.

So imagine my surprise, when on one of the most nerve-wracking days of my career, having made a call I had been putting off a very long time and leaving a seventeen-year tenure in favor of a "sue-battical" – my phone rang. It was none other than Carl himself.

Without a trace of call reluctance, Carl took the initiative to reach out to me on a personal level, simply to encourage me, lift me up, and offer support for my next steps. It blew me away. Shortly thereafter, having the chance to meet him and spend time at one of the live events when he showed me and the whole "Animals family" how to operate more effectively, blew me away once again.

Carl, Kevin and the Mortgage Marketing Animals team and family of clients are in a word, remarkable. They come together to learn, to support, to give. To share their mistakes and their wins. To detail out exactly what works and why. To look to the future and innovate together. And, with this book, you now have the opportunity to tap into those immeasurable years of experience and take the next step forward in your own journey.

You've already taken the first step and cracked the book open. Take another step, and dive in. You have nothing to lose, but you, your family and all those who have not yet had the pleasure of doing business with you have the world to gain. It might be uncomfortable here and there but don't stop – the best things in life are found outside of our comfort zone.

Keep going... and keep growing.

Sue Woodard

Mortgage Industry Expert | Chief Customer Officer, Total Expert

Table of Contents

Introduction: Welcome!

This book represents a lot of combined years (no need to say how many – just a lot!) of hard work, experience and effort from ourselves, our teams and our customers. You might even be one of them!

To clarify the core issue about call reluctance that we are talking about here can be summed it up in two sentences:

"Fear is peeing in your pants. Courage is doing what you need to do with wet pants on."

~ Carl White

Seriously, everybody feels the fear - truly everybody. You just can't create great results without standing on the edge. Even the most confident person you see on stage or that top producer who is making sales all day long on the phone may look fearless, but they're not. They feel the fear and do it anyway. They do what needs to be done with wet pants on.

This is truly the secret of all top producers of any industry. Being brave isn't supposed to be easy but it does get easier over time.

As you're reading this today, write down the three things that you've been wanting to do but where fear has held you back. Then ask yourself how much goodness you are procrastinating on and how much angst you cause yourself because you're not doing it. Finally, when you can see how your life would be that much better just to do those three things, feel the fear – and do them anyway. You'll be glad you did.

By the way, let's get one thing straight right here... this is NOT about shame or guilt. You always do the very best you can and, since call reluctance is a factor in your success, there's simply something that you don't yet know that can be the game-changer.

And THAT is the point of this book. By the time you finish reading here, you are going to have new insights, a fresh perspective, some tricks you can use to bypass your limiting beliefs and you will be able to pick up the phone and have conversations a whole lot easier.

In fact, while we're on the subject, one of the big keys to taming call reluctance – which is really picking up the phone to have a conversation with someone you may not know – is to remember that it's not about you. That call is about helping the person on the other end of the phone to have what they want – a solid mortgage opportunity. You are the messenger but you are NOT the message.

Take the spotlight off of you and shine it on the person you are getting ready to help. It's not about "You", it's about how you are going to help the person on the other end of the line. Perhaps you are going to be the only pleasant person they will be speaking to all day. Just keeping that in mind may be worth the price of admission in buying this book.

So here is what to expect in this book so you can get the most out of it.

First, you will discover opportunities to go deeper into the content, access free training materials and an interactive masterclass as well as join our online community as our guest.

Second, this book is for generating business. It is intended to help you neutralize or even overcome call reluctance so you can grow your business, generate qualified leads and close more deals faster and easier.

Third, this book is written for implementers. Nothing happens without action. If you're looking for a get-rich-quick scheme or free money, let us know when you find it! But seriously, this book is not for you if you're not prepared to act on what you learn. We are not known for blowing smoke and we are not going to start now – so you need to know the ideas in this book won't work unless you implement them.

Fourth, this book wasn't intended to be a #1 Bestseller (even if that ends up being the case). It's designed to start a conversation in writing so we can give you value, so you can get to know us and our approach, explore ideas you can use and, ultimately, help you decide if we will work together someday.

Fifth, this may be a short book but it is long on practical ideas you can implement right away. Our intention - the purpose of this book - is to show you what you can do and the mindset you need to neutralize call reluctance *pronto*. We have a how-to system to support you in doing just that based on what you learn here.

Are we going to invite you to do more? Heck yeah! We want to help you reach more people, help more people, make more money, add value to your life and to others around you! So you'll see opportunities throughout this book to watch videos or download PDFs and yes, we do have some great training that you can invest in to continue your new closing success momentum to have a better business, close more deals and make more money. We share what we know works and we will *enthusiastically* encourage you to check it all out!

Having said that, if you like what you read (or most of it), we want to hear from you, get to know you better and have you post a success story, picture or video and comment on our Facebook wall at Facebook.com/MortgageMarketingAnimals/ .

The BEST way to start or enhance a relationship with us is to visit the resources by using weblinks you find in this book, join the free training and learn more about how to overcome call reluctance so you can get and close more deals and, frankly, live your best life. It is our honor to help you help more people, make more money and live with more freedom every day!

Sincerely,

Carl White and Kevin Gillespie

P.S. – We decided that a done book was better than a perfect one so we wrote it fast and dirty. There could be spelling, grammar and layout mistakes in it. If you find an error, will you do us a favor and say what you find by sending an email to carl.white@themarketinganimals.com? Just note the page number, sentence and mistake so we can get that fixed right away and send you a gift for your help. We're all about results, getting you tools that make you money and value implementation – we live what we teach. So we're just doing it and asking that you help us make it better as you read it.

P.P.S. - If you love this book or make money because of it, will you please post a review here: CrushingCallReluctance.com/Review

If you DON'T like it, send us an email, say why and we'll give you your money back, ok?

In that case, be nice. We're giving you the best of what we know. We don't want your money if you're not thrilled with what you get out of this book. Our people – families, friends, colleagues and, of course, customers – read online reviews. There's no sense in dragging them through unnecessary drama. Nobody likes a bully. And we're all about live and let live. So no matter what, let's be friends, ok?

Thanks again for your support... now get ready to start making some calls and closing more deals!

Endorsements and Accolades

Carl and Kevin

"One of the biggest issues we've had at our organization was call reluctance, as I'm sure is common with a lot of companies. I pride myself on being a pretty darn good sales manager, or so I thought, then I attended one of Carl's call reluctance trainings. Two words - mind blown! I was able to come back to my team and completely retrain their mindset. Not only did their call reluctance become a thing of their past, but their conversions shot through the roof too! We literally went from not looking forward to making our calls to being absolutely stoked to make them! Big props to Carl and his training. Can't thank him enough."

~ **Frank Garay**, The National Real Estate Post

"I hated making calls. (I don't like calling anyone – even close friends!) Today I spoke with over 20 people, left messages for 20 more and it was great!

One of the things that kept me from picking up the phone was my hatred of surprises. (Surprises are great for birthdays, bad for mortgages!) Once I had a systemized plan, it was easy to pick up the phone because I knew what to say – the system gave me call scripts, which map out what to talk about and how the calls will go in advance. That gave me confidence.

Carl and Kevin and their team gave me a clear plan for any situation, making it easy to overcome the objections. I don't beat myself up when somebody says something negative - it's their issue, not mine, and it's a really rare occurrence anyway. The excellent news is that I have overcome my call reluctance and our team's business is growing exponentially as a result."
~**Jennifer Peterson Singh**, Poolesville, MD

"When I met you in 2014, I had major call reluctance. I knew I had to do something quick or get out of the business. So I attended one of your 3-day trainings. What I learned there is that people don't think about me like I

thought they did, so people don't finish a call with me and think I'm a jerk all day long. I really just had to overcome all the stuff in my head. Now I close a lot of loans because I don't have call reluctance anymore... I push through every day because I know that I bring a lot of value to my clients. I'm glad that I met you and took action to neutralize call reluctance – my family and my clients thank you for it!"
~**Ivan Acosta**, Colorado Springs, CO

"There were two big things that you taught me that helped me overcome my call reluctance: 1) positive self-talk in the morning to get my head in the right space so that I know the reason why I am making the calls, which is to grow my business so I can provide the life for my family that I want to, and 2) changing my mindset from selling someone to trying to build a relationship and possibly help them and not just trying to make a sale. When I do my self-talk and remind myself of that, I don't have any call reluctance at all. It's just when I forget to do those two things that I get off-track."
~ **Brian Kimball,** Nashville, TN

"Kevin has a unique ability to ease your fear and instill confidence in yourself."
~ **Stephen Roberts**, Austin, TX

Who Are We and Why Should You Listen to Or Trust Us?

We aren't the flashiest guys but we do know this industry and we keep it real when we teach our Mortgage Marketing Animals how to increase their monthly loan application volume. We have worked with thousands of loan officers who have claimed their readiness to help more people and live the lifestyle they want with the right income to support it.

Each of us came up in the business when there wasn't such a thing as social media or having a website. We didn't learn by having tools like that; instead, we had some pretty good motivation – like, feeding our families. And we had two options to use conversations to generate business – by putting our feet on the street and by calling people on the phone, networking at events, getting face to face appointments and any other way we could get a personal sales conversation going.

Now we want to take what we know how to do – generating sales volume through direct sales – to help loan officers like you get ahead. By making a simple mental shift, you can accelerate your results and change lives – yours and everyone's you touch through your business. And it can happen fast when you work with the system we're about to teach you.

Business loves speed. And doing deals means catching the opportunity in the moment. Catching those deals depends on talking to people, building relationships and being ready to help when the time is right. This book is focusing on neutralizing call reluctance which, really, is anything that prevents you from connecting with a prospect. So when we say 'phone', know that we are referencing the entire sphere by which you make contact with a potential buyer. By making the phone your new best friend, getting personal appointments and using a system to keep you on track, you may literally double your business in just eight weeks – as proven by our clients.

What would you rather do? Keep doing the same thing over and over, not getting the results you want, or transforming your relationship with call reluctance to become one of eager connection with your prospects and customers as the shortest path to your success?

That's what we're here to show you, based on what we know works in the real world. We'll share examples, exercises and strategies that can help you – IF you use them.

Here's to transforming call reluctance into call revelation so you can grow your business by helping more people!

Overview and Explanation of This Book

How much do you think call reluctance is costing you?

Is it just a dollar amount or something more? Is it costing you the lifestyle you want? Is it robbing you of having more of what you want? Maybe it's taking time away from your family and loved ones...

The point is that call reluctance is insidious. Every day that goes by it's easy to think that tomorrow is another day... and then tomorrow is another day to make those calls... no, really, tomorrow will be the day. Every day that call reluctance has the power to knock you back from making those calls is a day that someone is missing out on a great mortgage opportunity and, as a result, your life pays the price. Yes, it's about money but, ultimately, this is about you having the life you deserve.

Let's really drive this home... what's the number one reason you're not producing the volume and making the income you want?

It's straight-forward... say it with us... call reluctance!

BUT here's the great news – call reluctance is the one thing you can overcome that can make a huge difference (financially and personally) in your life.

Let's begin by roughing out some basic goals. The first thing you need to figure out is how much money do you need. What's your dream house? What's your dream vacation? How much do you want to save for your kid's college fund? How much do you want to save for a rainy day? What is your electric bill? Do a breakdown of what your perfect life would be and put a price tag on it.

The good thing about loan officers is we make good money every time somebody says yes. It's not like an hourly job where you're making minimum wage or even when you sell a book and make about $3 by the time it's all said and done. Every time a loan officer gets money, when someone says, "Yeah, man - I'll take that deal," they are on average bringing in about $2,000. That might be a low average, but let's just say that's average - about $2,000.

Whatever you're starting at, we only need another five loans a month - which is not hard - to make another $10k a month. It's impressive. Once you figure out how much money you need to have your dream life, how many deals you need to make that happen, how many loans you need per month to make your dream life a reality, you've got good intel. Because then you play the averages.

On average, about one out of every four referrals close, so if you get four people referred to you and you get them on the phone, the odds are in your favor because you're going to close at least one of them. That is an industry standard – an average closing rate of 25%.

So now the math gets easy. How many leads do you need if you want to close another five loans? You only need 20 leads. That's like nothing for somebody who picks up the phone.

Now, there is a difference in the source of the lead because a phone lead is light years better than an internet lead. Let's acknowledge that fact.

But, in any case, once you know how many leads you need to get that many closings, to make that much money to have your perfect life, how much prospecting do you need to do to get those many leads? Just follow the dots to come up with your numbers.

It's ok if you don't pick up the phone today...

Now, it's okay if you don't pick up the phone today. Said with love, just get out your little black marker and cross through that vacation. Mark through the savings for your family to leave as a legacy. Mark through the college fund for the kids.

This isn't about shame or guilt! This is about the power of choice that you have today – right now – right in front of you.

It's okay to not pick up the phone - just be prepared to have that conversation with your loved ones. "Hey Bobby, I've decided not to pick up a phone today. So we need to cross off that money for your college fund. We're X-ing through that vacation that we've always wanted to take to Yellowstone, or see Rome, or whatever."

Let's keep going... (now this is a little painful but it's the reality – we gotta keep it real)... "We're going to mark through getting that new car for my spouse – the one that's taken care of the yard or washed my underwear for the last 35 years. We're going to mark through giving my wife that weekly pedicure that she is so worthy of… or my husband's dream riding mower or the boat that we both want."

It's okay to not pick up the phone – you just have to recognize you're making a choice. You either A: pick a phone or B: pick up a black marker and start crossing off parts of your best life. Either way, it doesn't take away the fear – but you're choosing to let fear be bigger than you in having your best life.

Remember, many people never get over the fear of picking up the phone – they just learn to do it with their wet pants on. But we're thinking that you could be the superstar that proves that wrong… you can be the one to completely neutralize call reluctance and power up your phone conversations so you can close more deals faster and easier!

And that's what this book is about… changing the way you do business by giving you ways to minimize, neutralize or even eliminate call reluctance.

Challenges in picking up the phone

Every loan officer needs to get and close deals as quickly as possible but usually have these challenges when it comes to picking up the phone (how many of these sounds like you?):

- You think you're going to get rejected.
- You worry about putting your reputation on the line.
- In your deepest core, you think sales is smarmy.
- The stress is unbearable so, of course, everyone else knows you feel out of control.
- You worry about striking out.
- You don't have time to make calls.
- You can't call from a loud environment but it's too late to call people by the time you get to your office.
- Your heart beats so fast you think you're going to keel over.
- You don't know if you can talk louder than the thoughts in your head telling you that you can't do this.
- You're worried you won't know what to say if someone actually picks up.
- You don't know where to find good quality leads.
- You feel pressure to *get this deal NOW.*

This system is the solution for all these challenges because it will give you practical ways to handle calls with confidence. Why is that so important? Phone calls:

- Don't require an advertising budget.
- Don't need a lot of time to set up your calls.
- Don't need employees or help to get them done.
- Don't require that you master some special technology.
- Can close deals of any size – because it all starts with a conversation.

We are going to give you some context for sales as well as some key research that may surprise you about why phone calls for sales are perceived to be so challenging. You're going to see the excuses and distractions that, when in the light of day, don't hold water as a reason to stop you from making calls. You're going to get a powerhouse, yet simple, system by which to manage your phone calls to make it ridiculously easy to just do them. And you're going to learn that your biology has programmed some of your responses so there will be some tools to help you manage that too.

Let's begin with something that is deceptively simple but oh-so-profound in helping you transform your relationship with sales calls...

Think of Small as Big

When we talk about the number one reason people aren't producing the volume they want in their business and making the kind of income they want - especially after setting goals — it usually comes down to a couple of things. One is not having the right support team. Another is thinking you need to know everything before you pick up the phone. And one of the major hurdles is not recognizing that the 80 / 20 rule is real, meaning that 80% of your results come from 20% of your actions.

The good news in that is that you can create more significant results by focusing on the 20% of your business activities that yield big results. What is that, you're asking? You already know but we'll cut to the chase — picking up the phone and talking to more people every day. THAT's the 20%!

We've been doing this work for decades now and we've seen more good-looking, sharp, articulate, intelligent sales people — people who are 10x more knowledgeable than us! — who, behind the scenes, struggle just to make a living.

Now, something that we are really good at is sheer persistence. We might not be the best-lookin' or sharpest-dressed guys – but we don't know how to give up. And we do know how to have real conversations with people. We are absolutely committed to bringing value to our customers and we don't let the phone be bigger than we are in our business. That's what we're talking about here – making the phone an instrument of your ability to help people live better lives vs. letting it control you through fear or intimidation. The phone needs to be your best friend.

Business happens one conversation at a time. We have a group of mortgage loan officers – the Freedom Club for Loan Officers – who are dedicated to helping people have the homes and, as a result, the lives they want to have every day. In this group, we looked at what this group and what producers at different companies were doing in terms of getting results. Here's what we found.

Four producer profiles

Basically, there's the 15% of producers who aren't doing much of anything – maybe they're beginners or maybe they're just not motivated enough to get it in gear. Then there's the 65% - we'll call them the average population –

are producing a couple of loans a month. They're probably doing $500k in monthly volume. By the way, the typical average "reasonably good" producer in the U.S. does about $700,000 a month and probably making around $70/year. Now that's respectable! And, if they're good, they'll bring in about $100k/ year.

Then there are the producers we labelled 'professional' who are generating more than $1.5 million / month in volume. And the 'elite' producers are generating more than $3 million / month, some in our group do 20 million or more per month in personal loan production (not counting other LOs in their branch).

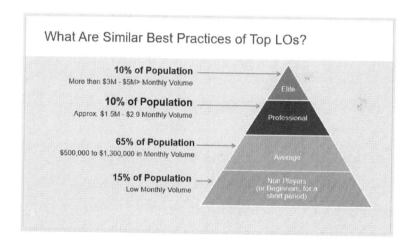

So what are the elite producers doing differently? Everybody has the same 24 hours in a day, right? Some people might think these top producers have a special website or they're connected to a builder or they have an uncle who owns a brokerage but that isn't it at all.

Amazingly, the big difference we found was in how they spend their time. When you ask these elite producers about their activity, they're having 50-plus good conversations on the phone a week, and then they're having typically 10 - 15 face-to-face meetings a week. That is the driver of their results.

Most average loan officers will say they're working about 40 hours / week – and so do the elite. The difference is the elite spend most of their time prospecting. They have their office set up so that they can be selling most of the time. One of the strategies we teach in the Freedom Club is how to build a system where you hire people – build your team – so you can be selling from your office chair.

To show you just how important it is to increase your prospecting time, check out this graph that shows that each of our four groups of producers are working the same number of hours – BUT focus a greater percentage of their time in prospecting. Look at what it does to their income each month. And that makes sense, right? More leads will, ultimately, result in more deals done which generates more income for that producer.

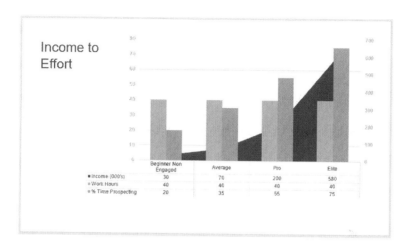

We call it the correlation of 'income to effort' when it comes to making calls. For example, a beginner may spend only 20% of their time prospecting and earn an average of $30,000per year for a 40-hour week. Jump to the elite earners and you'll find that they spend 75% of their time prospecting. As a result, their income catapults to an average of $580,000 per year while working about the same amount of hours per week - or even less hours per week!

Go linebacker

Here's a quick story for you about a loan officer in one of our groups who has become a dear friend to us and a shining example of what happens when you just pick up the phone. When he came to us, he was closing maybe one deal every six months - you got it, two loans per YEAR. Now, like me, he may not be the most socially savvy guy... in fact, he's very introverted. But, after working together with us for a while, he now picks up the phone and he has months when he'll close 10, 11, 12 deals! He's gone from 2 a year to close to 100 per year. That's a life-changing 50X increase for him. It puts him in the top high percentage of producer-earners in the nation. In his slow months, he'll close five or six.

Here's the thing – he holds three records in our group: 1) he holds, by percentage, the largest increase in his business from when he started to where he is now (50X increase), 2) he holds the record of making the most calls, and, 3) he holds the record of getting the most "no's". So when he picks up the phone to make calls for meetings with agents, which is a deceptively simple strategy for getting referrals, he holds the record for making the most phone calls and hearing the most no's. Despite his challenged disposition, he picks up the phone like a linebacker. And he's doing well for himself and his customers.

That brings us to another small thing that makes a big difference and, sometimes, it's something that handsome, pretty people need to overcome to be successful... and that is being used to hearing the word no. Attractive people find that they can cut in lines, doors are opened for them and they can wear a burlap sack and still look good... they have a lot of yes's in life. But that means they can be more challenged when it comes to hearing no, which is the symptom of being a lead generator. You may not ever have thought about that before and that's the point of this book – to challenge your thinking about what you think you know to help you become a higher-producing loan officer.

~~~~~

Key Takeaways:

- You can create more significant results in your business by focusing on the 20% of activities that yield big results.
- Make the phone an instrument of your ability to help people live better.
- Business happens one conversation at a time.

- Elite producers have 50+ good conversations on the phone a week, and then 10 - 15 face-to-face meetings a week; this combination drives their results.
- The correlation of 'income to effort' means more leads will, ultimately, result in more deals done which generates more income for that producer.
- Lead generators hear "no" more often – it's the sign that means they will, eventually, have more business.

A quick note here - if you are wondering how these elite producers have time to make that many phone calls and face-to-face meetings a week instead of putting out fires all day long, we can discuss team-building on your free bonus call that you are making with us. Schedule yours now: CrushingCallReluctance.com/Call

The Law of Large Numbers

One more concept to help set the context here... the Law of Large Numbers.

Essentially, the Law states that the more conversations, face-to-face weekly meetings, events and meals you have, the higher your production results. Just a small shift in how many connections you have with your prospects can yield significant results.

Law of Large Numbers

What would this sort of activity do to your business?

	Day of High Producer	Week	90 Days	Annually
Conversations/Week	10>	50	600	2,100
Face to Face Meetings/Week	3	15	180	720
Events	--	1	12	50
Meals	1	5	60	240

Most loan officers think that their skill level is what changes their income but that is not true. In fact, the highest indicator of sales success is lead development and

Get the Free Bonus- CrushingCallReluctance.com/Call

prospecting. You can take classes and seminars but, unless you prospect well to generate leads, your business will not grow. So it's not about what you know as much as it is about how many people who know that you know it.

The bottom line is that if you don't contact a whole lot of people, all the techniques, tactics and strategies won't produce results. You can have the perfect system in place but, if you don't make the calls, you won't do the business. And if you screw everything else but you DO make the calls, you're still going to have success.

Large numbers in action

When loan officers in the Freedom Club start making calls, where the average person starts out making 10 calls / day (M-F) and sets a couple of appointments, everything changes. In just 90 days, that person will have had 600 conversations and 180 face-to-face meetings. In that environment, you don't have to be a great salesperson – the law of averages is on your side.

It's like the casinos, where they get the law of averages on their side by manipulating the environment. There's loud noises, and no clocks, and they're pumping oxygen in with pretty fragrances in the air. They're doing everything to keep you in the casino and the odds are in their favor. That's what making these calls is – it puts the odds in your favor. Even if you're not an awesome salesperson, you're going to find some people who like and trust you, and who are going to do business with you. It just works.

How to predict your future

Here's a way to predict your future... it's the 30-90 rule. Whatever you do in this 30-day period is going to determine what you're making 90 days from now.

Now, some people will confuse putting the odds in their favor with busy work. Busy work looks like buying market leads, putting up a fancy website, getting busy on social media... but these only look efficient because the motivation behind them is that the loan officer is looking for a silver bullet so they don't have to pick up the phone.

Essentially, there is an internal issue that means the loan officer is not changing their mindset or behavior to being successful. It could be call resistance, or approval addiction, or fear of rejection – whatever the label, it means that the loan officer is not promoting the value of their service to the people who might need it or know someone who needs it. In other words, they need to become better self-promoters.

Look at Oprah Winfrey, Donald Trump, Kevin Hart... consider all the top sales people and event promoters and Hollywood moguls – they are self-promoters. They have the confidence to make the calls. The ones who don't have that confidence you don't hear about because they're not making the calls. Their addiction to "being validated by others" is bigger than their need to serve and help others get what they want and, truthfully, 95% of people have this to some degree – but the truly successful get through it.

> ❝
> The average sales person works less than 1.5 hours a day in actual sales prospecting activity. ❞
>
> Bill Grimes

Those successful people also spend most of their time in cultivating relationships. According to Bill Grimes, who works with stock brokers in Oklahoma, says that the average salesperson spends less than 90 minutes a day on prospecting. Its' been our experience that the average loan officer spends 0 hours prospecting... that's right, ZERO. You can see from what we shared about elite loan officers that they are spending 5 – 6 hours / day on prospecting and relationship cultivation. That alone demonstrates the difference between the average and the elite professional.

Do you have call reluctance?

So how do you know if you have call reluctance? Ask and answer honestly the following two questions.

• Have you had 12-15 face-to-face appointments in the past week?

• In the past several weeks, have you made 50 contacts or more?

If your answers are "No," then you likely have call reluctance.

Of course, you can also realize you have resistance to calling when you experience these physical symptoms:
• Talk louder and faster.
• Experience heart rate increase (even pounding!).

• Perspire more.

• Have "butterflies."

• Experience tightness in the chest.

• Have a hard time remembering key points and what you planned to say.

• Experience a higher pitch in your voice.

The good news is that you can use these symptoms as a barometer to know exactly when it's time to pump up your confidence and spring into action. Why? Because fear can only show up when you are in action. So the act of prospecting is, ironically, the cure for call reluctance.

One other way you can see if you have call reluctance is to just check your bank balance. If you aren't comfortable with what you see there, call reluctance is probably a major factor in your daily activities.

~~~~~

Key Takeaways:

- The Law of Large Numbers states that the more conversations, face-to-face weekly meetings, events and meals you have, the higher your production results.

- A small shift in how many connections you have with your prospects can yield significant positive returns in your business.
- The highest indicator of sales success is not sales skill but lead development and prospecting.
- You can have the perfect system in place but, if you don't make the calls, you won't do the business. And if you screw everything else but you DO make the calls, you're still going to have success.
- You can activate the Law of Averages in just 90 days to help build your business by having 600 conversations and 180 face-to-face meetings.
- You can predict your future with the 30-90 rule. Whatever you do in this 30-day period is going to determine what you're making 90 days from now.
- Loan officers need to become better self-promoters.
- Elite loan officers spend 5 – 6 hours / day on prospecting and relationship cultivation.
- Fear can only show up when you are in action. So the act of prospecting is, ironically, the cure for call reluctance.

The Not-So-Secret Secret

Perception is everything. How you perceive the world around you will determine the quality of your life and business experience. Every human learns how to perceive the world as a child, through parents and authority figures who say 'here's what to believe' and then act as role models in living those perceptions. Most people never objectively question their perceptions – which become beliefs over time – to make sure they really do believe them. And yet, those perceptions are what create their life and business as it is today.

How does that relate to call reluctance? Well, call reluctance is an old perception that became a habit – as a coping mechanism, in a way – that has its roots in trying to protect you from rejection or humiliation. Somewhere in life, you perceived that picking up the phone could result in a negative experience for you. So call reluctance looks like thoughts, feelings, perceptions, choices and behaviors that keep a loan officer (or any salesperson, really) from picking up that phone.

Additionally, being human means that we want to believe we are right in what we know so we look for ways to prove ourselves right. Of course, this reinforces that what we already know is the 'right' way to perceive our experience. We work from what is right (by what we know) vs. what is possible (what we don't know). It's one way to live in a comfort zone, which was the ultimate destination for our ancestors for thousands of years – living in safety from predators, unexpected danger and unpredictable results.

That means, essentially, you are challenging your own biology every time you go to pick up that phone. Why? Because the primitive warning system of your brain – your amygdala – is programmed to look for anything unfamiliar that might put you in harm's way, which looks like doing something new, unfamiliar or unexpected, and stop it.

For example, when you want to lose weight and you decide to work out, eat right and sleep more, you probably find that's exactly when you want to get a pizza. It's because your amygdala comes in and sabotages those new behaviors to keep you in a stable, known condition (even if that's not what you want). Too many changes at once will kick your amygdala into gear and shut down what it perceives as danger.

This same mechanism is activated when you do something new, that might put you at risk socially (of rejection or humiliation), or that has big ramifications on your future (in case it doesn't work out). Some might call this approval addiction, where some part of you needs to know that you are validated for what you know. Freud called it the death wish - the internal destructive force that arises whenever we choose a long-term course of action that may do us or others good.

Some have called this behavior 'learned helplessness', which happens when a person who is forced to endure something unpleasant decides they cannot repeat that same thing again because they have learned they cannot control the situation and don't want to feel that unpleasant thing again.

Steven Pressfield, the author of Bagger Vance (if you remember that book or movie), wrote a book about resistance and the fears we have that we further interpret into call reluctance. In our minds, call reluctance is a form of resistance and a signal for the fears we have resulting in self-corruption, which is self-sabotage in the highest degree against the person having what they want, which results in procrastination. It stunts us and makes us less than what we're meant to be. Procrastination is simply delaying the result that someone, ultimately, wants to experience. So when you are procrastinating on picking up that phone, you're just delaying what you want and corrupting your ability to have the life you really want as an everyday reality. The definition of safety here is based on the history of what you have experienced vs. something new and, by definition, unknown.

There was a 30-year study done by a couple of researchers (Dudley and Goodson) that summarized call reluctance as 'all the thoughts, feelings and avoidance behaviors that conspire to keep otherwise talented, motivated and high-potential sales people from earning what they are worth'. So if you aren't earning what you are worth, it's probably call reluctance that's getting in your way.

Jung said, "When an inner situation is not made conscious, it appears outside of you as fate.". The good news is that you obviously don't accept that because you are reading this book right now to create transformation that will have a positive effect on your business. That is the real power of humanity in action right there – choosing something different in the face of all the reasons why your biology wants you to stay right where you are to keep you safe in your comfort zone. Comfort zones can be prisons of our own making, right?

And that is also the not-so-secret secret – that to create change, you're going to have to do something different. To break out of established patterns and habits, you need a way to go beyond where you've always been or you'll just keep getting the same results.

It's interesting when we go in and do a presentation to loan officers and we will ask, "*How many of you have 10 to 15 appointments scheduled for next week?*" Literally, maybe one out of 100 will raise their hand. Then we'll extend that timeframe and ask, "*How many of you in the last couple of weeks have been on 10 or 15 appointments, and made 50 calls?*" Nobody raises their hands.

The big discovery here is that <u>to have different results, you're going to have to do something different.</u> What got you 'here' will not get you 'there'. Call reluctance has outlived its usefulness – it cannot rule your business anymore. It is literally robbing you of claiming your power to have the life you want and to help others have what they want too.

The spin doctor

Your mind is a spin doctor. It has no conscience. Simply put, your brain is designed to keep you from changing. So, it's going to tell you anything you want to hear - that these emails are more important, or I've got to do this, or I've got to do that — just to get you to stay where you are, where it perceives you as safe. It's going to lie to you and you'll say, "Well, I'll start tomorrow and then it will start all over again." It will do anything to keep you from making your calls. It's your subconscious mind.

From a psychological standpoint, remember that all your behavior is controlled by your beliefs. Beliefs create your feelings and your certainty. The emotions that your beliefs create result in your actions. And your beliefs may or may not be good for you, by the way. Tony Robbins says, "*A belief is nothing more than certainty within your nervous system.*" So you have things you know but then you also have things you really believe... and it's those things that you really believe that stop you.

By looking at how you were raised, could you have beliefs, whether conscious or unconscious, about relationships and acceptance and rejection? One theory says that's in your DNA because, historically over generations, you had to be accepted by the tribe to survive. If you weren't accepted by the tribe, they shunned you and you were sent out into the wilderness to fend for yourself. So, you had to fit in or risk death.

In society today, growing up in most families means you have to watch your P's and Q's and be polite. You probably learned that it's rude if you're asking people too many questions, or interrupting them, or talking to them all the time. As a kid, you think quick and you figure out that your parents are saying, "*I don't want to hear it from you unless you're spoken to, or kids are meant to be seen and not heard.*" Those are the situations that form our beliefs that build us into who we are today.

On top of that, we learn that relationships are very hard, and it's hard to ask for what you want. And in school, you probably didn't get promoted for speaking out in class or talking (which is what sales is all about); instead, you were told to sit there and be quiet and always have the right answer. (And in sales, we don't always have the right answer.) Of course, your friends did a real nice job of picking on you and making you feel like you weren't part of the clique or whatever, which triggers that primal fear of being banished to the wilderness to live on your own.

The point is we have all these things in our upbringing about how we think relationship should be and, unfortunately, as we become adults, we're still tied to them. As a kid, emotional situations seem like a bigger deal. Over time, as you mature, you can handle them differently – but you're still relating to them as you learned to do when you were a kid.

For example, there was a study by the University of Michigan that showed when we're rejected, the brain puts out opiates as if you're physically hurt. You can see this when somebody has been in a car accident. They go into shock. People ask, "*hey, are you ok? You better go to the hospital.*" But they say, "*No, I'm okay. I'm okay.*" They just shove it off but they're in shock. Their mind is pumping opiates to protect them. And then, the next day, they wake up and realize they're hurt and they should have gone to the hospital. It's literally a psychological and biological protection mechanism in that moment.

Today that happens to us but in a different way. Today it includes more than physical injury or trauma – it includes image, reputation acceptance, being liked and social rejection. We're going to cover how our conscious and subconscious mind works to handle this protection mechanism and how that affects being a loan officer later in this book. For now, here's the big question:

With the reward being your happiness, freedom and having the life and business you want on your own terms, what would it be worth to you to finally resolve call reluctance?

The answer to that question will pull you through making it happen.

~~~~~

Key Takeaways:

- How you perceive the world around you will determine the quality of your life and business experience.
- Most people never objectively question their perceptions and beliefs to make sure they really do believe them. And yet, those are the very things that create their life and business as it is today.
- Call reluctance is an old perception that became a habit, from a coping mechanism, that has its roots in trying to protect you from rejection or humiliation.

- We work from what is right (by what we know) vs. what is possible (what we don't know).
- You are challenging your own biology — your primitive brain's warning system — every time you go to pick up that phone.
- Approval addiction happens when some part of you needs to know that you are validated for what you know.
- Call reluctance is a form of resistance and a signal for the fears we have resulting in self-corruption, which is self-sabotage in the highest degree against the person having what they want, which results in procrastination.
- If you aren't earning what you are worth, it's probably call reluctance that's getting in your way.
- To create change, you're going to have to do something different or you'll just keep getting the same results.
- Call reluctance is literally robbing you of having the life you want and helping others have what they want too.
- Your brain is designed to keep you from changing to keep you in the safety of the 'known'.
- You have things you know but then you also have things you really believe... and it's those things that you really believe that stop you.

Bonus Quiz: What's Your Level of Call Reluctance?

Take this quiz and find out!

Please answer the following questions as honestly as you can to learn just how much call reluctance is holding you back in living the life you really want.

Place a mark next to each statement that is true for you as of today. If the statement does not apply or will/cannot be true for you, leave it blank as no / false. Total the number of marks for the yes / true statements. Then add the marks for a total score. At the end, you will learn what your score means. Good luck!

____ I have used at least one of these statements in the last 30 days to describe why my business isn't closing more deals: "it's the market", "it's the time of the year" and/or "it's the underwriters".

____ I have too many things to do by the time I get around to picking up the phone so I don't get the calls made that I want (and then I don't want to take time away from my family).

_____ I find it challenging and awkward to ask for referrals from people I know.

_____ I just know people can tell I'm nervous when I call - I feel out of control - so I can't make as many calls as I want every day.

_____ I worry that I won't know what to say when someone actually picks up the phone.

_____ In the past week, I have had less than 10 phone conversations with prospects.

_____ In the past week, I have had less than 8 face-to-face appointments with prospects.

_____ I can't make calls from the road or loud environments, like when I'm networking, and it's too late to make calls by the time I get to my office.

_____ I don't know where to find good quality leads for calls.

_____ In the past week, I have had less than 10 phone conversations with prospects.

_____ I have contacts I previously called that I haven't called back since the first conversation with them.

_____ I only work by incoming referrals.

_____ In the last 30 days, I have thought this at least once: "If I call that person, s/he is probably already working with or knows somebody else – I don't want to step on their toes or be too pushy."

_____ In the last 30 days, I have thought this at least once: "I don't want to make that call yet because I don't know enough and/or I don't feel confident."

_____ In the last 30 days, I have thought this at least once: "I don't want to influence somebody into making a decision they might not be ready for or be pushy / aggressive / intrusive."

_____ I want my prospects to be my friends so they think of me when they're ready to buy.

_____ If I go out make a lot of calls and people tell me no, it must mean I'm not in control.

_____ When I make calls, I talk louder and faster, my heart rate increases, I sweat, have butterflies, my chest gets tight, I forget what I was going to say and/or my voice goes squeaky.

_____ I worry about striking out or being rejected.

_____ I worry about putting my reputation on the line. I mean, what if the deal doesn't work out right?

Tally how many marks you have checked above; out of 20 questions, how many are marked?

Take your total number and multiply it by 5 – this will give you the percentage (out of 100%) of how much call reluctance is holding you back. For example, if you checked 10 answers, multiplied by 5, you get 50 – so call reluctance is holding you back in business by a factor of 50%.

Now, you may find that call reluctance is a significant issue and, in that case, congratulations! You've identified something that, when handled simply and easily with our system, will shift quickly and your business will skyrocket as a result.

If you, instead, learned that call reluctance really isn't that big a deal for you, congratulations! And... you need to stretch your comfort zones even further to get bigger, better results. (We can help you with that too.)

Either way, whatever you learn here gives you more information about yourself and how much call reluctance is holding back your business.

And, either, way, remember that your application volume and business can grow faster and easier by using our proven system to make a mindset shift and then a behavior shift. Like we have already mentioned, in just 12 weeks, we have had students double (and more!) their application volume.

What's Your Self-Image?

We need to talk about the characteristics of top earners and their attitudes toward making calls to help you reshape your self-image as a top earner. When you know what it looks like, it's easier to achieve.

The average loan officer tends to tell themselves that their call reluctance is due to external factors – "it's the market...it's the time of the year... it's the underwriters", etc.

However, the truth is that call reluctance is internal. It's the emotional hesitation that causes you to:
• Avoid making contacts.
• Avoid asking for the business.
• Avoid asking for referrals.

But the elite producers neutralize this emotional hesitation. We know that because we surveyed four top earners (BK, LW, CJ and MS) in different markets, with different personalities and even selling different product lines. What we found was astounding in that none of that made any difference; instead, these top earners all shared one key distinguishing factor that was consistent across the board.

And that distinguishing factor is what you can see from the following chart – they did a minimum of 50 conversations and 15 face-to-face meetings per week. They also tried to do at least one event per week and one had meals with their potential customers. This activity generated approximately $21 million in monthly volume from just four elite producers, or an average of $5.4M per month EACH. The key to making these kinds of results happen? Doing it consistently, week in – week out, without hesitation.

Top Income Earners Focus On Lead Development And Number Of Contacts They Make Each Week!

	BK WI	LW MN	CJ FL	MS FL	Low Side of the Curve
Average Monthly Volume	$5.02M	$6.89M	$3.8M	$5.92M	$5.4M
Conversations/Week	50	60	60	60	50
Face to Face Meetings/Week	15	17	15	15	15
Events	1	0.5	1	1-2	1
Meals	5				5

Then we did another test of twelve different producers. We took a baseline on the calls they were making each week, and then we gave them an 8-week training and call scripts to use in their business. At the end of that experiment, three producers dropped out (and sadly chose to be satisfied with what they weren't satisfied with...) so we had nine finish the program.

Of those nine individuals, all saw similar results. They started at doing about 15 calls / week; once we got them up to doing about 50 calls / week and getting their appointments to over 10 per week, we saw their application volume more than double – in just eight weeks.

Over the course of a year, that's about 2,100 conversations that are directed toward building relationships. There is statistically no way that your business would NOT see an epic difference when you are having that many conversations with people about helping them have what they really want through your help. Essentially, it's a numbers game because not everybody can reject you 100% of the time.

Quick truth point: How would that kind of income change your life? What changes would you be willing to make if you could double your application volume in just 60 days?

Test

J A – WI	Average Start	6-Apr	13-Apr	20-Apr	27-Apr	4-May	11-May	18-May		Weekly Ave	Total
Calls	15	51	57	51	55	32	33	50			
Appts	3	13	19	16	13	16	22	11			
Prequals	3	3	7	3	7	4	5	6			
Apps	2	3	5	3	5	4	4	6		4.3	30

J M – TN	Average Start	6-Apr	13-Apr	20-Apr	27-Apr	4-May	11-May	18-May		Weekly Ave	Total
Calls	20	52	30	36	59	55	53	51			
Appts	1.5	6	6	6	7	13	6	7			
Prequals	3	9	4	6	7	6	7	7			
Apps	2	6	0	2	8	5	6	5		4.6	32

Results from two of the nine program participants

So the kind of change we are talking about here in handling call reluctance can yield quick results. Focusing on how to handle your call reluctance and increase your appointments is the number one thing you can do to positively impact your bottom-line in your business!

Maintaining call momentum

The other thing we found is that the follow-through these elite producers did in terms of their calls made a significant positive difference. Here's what we know: 44% of loan officers will give up after the first call and 22% after the second.

We also know that higher lead generation creates increased follow-through. For example, on the first call to clients, only 5% of sales are made - on the second call, it's

12% and on the third, 18%. But once you make that fourth call, then results really start to happen. The fourth call rises to 30% of sales made, and on the fifth call it goes up to 35%.

That means 66% of loan officers give up after just the second contact while, at the same time, more than 80% of the relationships are not built until after that point in the follow-through cycle.

In the Freedom Club, we teach that you need to call your referral partner prospects weekly for up to 12 weeks to get an appointment. And then you may need to call for another 12 weeks after that to get the first closable referral. Now, we find that results typically happen faster than that but with that kind of commitment, we are not about to give up. And when our student loan officers' percentages of success increase, they don't either! But we find most loan officers don't even make the first or second call and those that do, well, most of them give up too soon too!

Contacts vs Sales Made

	1st Call	2nd Call	3rd Call	4th Call	5th> Call
▪ When sales are made	5%	12%	18%	30%	35%
▪ Sales People Who Give Up	44%	22%	14%	12%	8%

One of the (many) value-adds of our program is that we show loan officers how to add value with each of the times they call with various strategies we teach. That gives them a reason to call so it feels more natural to continue the momentum and pace they're setting with their calls.

To ride the wave of increased volume means building relationships over time with multiple touchpoints. Just think about how you do business with someone new – do you buy what they're selling after the first call?

Two categories of sales people

Let's talk about two categories, or profiles, of behaviors that call out how insidious call reluctance can be in practical terms. We call these the Sales Snob and the Performance Anxiety Individuals.

The Sales Snob

The Sales Snob unconsciously thinks that sales is a bad thing. They think sales is beneath them and, probably, it was their parents who gave them that idea. Their parents might have said things like, 'watch out for that guy – he's trying to sell you something'.

For them, it's about social hierarchy and status. Do they live on the right side of the tracks? Do they belong to the right country club? Do they go to the right restaurants? Are they seen in the right places? (Growing up, the only way we got be in the country club was to be the caddie or the busboy!)

But sometimes, especially when someone grew up in a not-so-wealthy family, they will do the cover-up. They want to be accepted. So the Sales Snob hides behind an image façade - they're dressed to kill, have the nicest office, drive the nicest car, etc. And a lot of us will go into sales because we like all those nice, bright, shiny objects. The difference is that the Sales Snob thinks if they put on this image of being successful, then they will get more business. But that isn't true. There is not one time that either of us has gotten a loan because somebody walked in and said, "Oh my God, look at this office" - it just doesn't happen. Even worse, when Sales Snobs have call reluctance, then they probably can't afford all those nice things and they're living beyond their means.

Sales Snobs will say things like, "I only work by referral." Well, to work by referral only, you have had to have done a lot of business and have a big database of people. The only way that's possible is when that person has been out selling. But the Sales Snob unconsciously feels like they're ashamed to be in sales so that isn't usually the case.

Now here is an interesting reality in our business. The truth is that loan offers are sales people going to real estate agents - who are sales people - to get business from them. Now, a Sales Snob might say "I don't want to sound sales-y" but you have two sales people, the loan officer and the real estate agent, talking together. That would be like getting two football players together and saying, "Dude, I don't want to sound football-y so let's not talk about football."

The fear of 'sales-y' is that sales has gotten a negative connotation. There's a stigma associated with sales – just think about how most people relate to car salespeople. But that response has been conditioned over time by people being pummeled by an unsophisticated, non-consultive salesperson.

To get out of this trap, the Sales Snob has to overcome their social conditioning and shift their attitude from 'sales is bad' to 'sales is helping people'. For example, if you have a flat tire on your car and you go to the tire store, and the salesperson sells you a tire, they're not selling you – they're solving your problem. They're helping you get what you want.

And as loan officers, we're not just helping the buyers but we're also helping the real estate agents to get a great loan so they can make their living too. We're helping families move into homes where they can build their dreams. We're helping communities build infrastructure and tax base. We have the most honorable profession in the world and, when Sales Snobs make that connection, the sky's the limit for them.

"Performance Anxiety" Individuals

This category includes people who are afraid they'll screw it all up and be rejected. There are four 'flavors' of this category as follows.

• **Danny/Debbie Downers**, who constantly anticipate a disaster instead of success. They'll act positive but, in their head, they're thinking, "*Man, if I call that person, s/he is probably already working with somebody, or s/he knows somebody. Or if I call, I'll just get their voicemail. Why should I call them?*"

• **Know It All's**, who have to have all the answers so they over-prepare. They spend so much time getting ready to get ready that they're not out there making sales! They think, "*I don't want to go do that call yet because I don't know enough. I don't want to go make those sales calls until I get this presentation perfectly right or until I get that piece of information.*"

• **BFFs**, who tend to have their foot on the brakes all the time. They don't want to feel aggressive so they're just constantly being nice and not asking for the business. They just want to be best friends forever. They think, "*I* don't want to be pushy or aggressive or intrusive. I don't want to influence somebody into making a decision — I just want to be nice and I want us to just be friends so they think of me when they're ready to buy."

• **Control Freaks**, who are so focused on finding exactly the right tool (new website, social strategy, etc.) that they don't actually get out to make calls and increase their business. They think, "*If I go out make a lot of calls and people tell me no, it must mean I'm not in control.*"

Here's the thing... a lot of us become loan officers because we think, "*Hey, I like working with people. I like being social. I like talking, and visiting, and helping people, and loan officers do this.*" It's almost like if that's what you like to do, and then you go out and you get all these no's, it's going against the very grain of who you are as a person internally. So, for Performance Anxiety Individuals, you have a counterbalance in that every "no" meets an inner compulsion that says, "*No way. That can't be right. People like me. I'm used to people liking me.*" And that belief is really kind of an anchor around making more calls.

We say that to tame performance anxiety means removing the fear of potentially striking out and getting more time at bat. Just like in baseball, where they track the batting average on home runs and on strike-outs, the only way to get sales up is to have more touch points with prospects. It's about showing up more often. It's about not letting the distractions take over. And it's about not giving in to the immediate gratifications of whatever is more enjoyable than what we need to be doing in the moment.

The creative excuses

Of course, there are all kinds of excuses we tend to come up with to avoid making calls. We're all talented like that. These excuses include:

• Email

• Phone interruptions

• File problems

• Office issues

• System problems

• That "next great strategy" or "shiny whistle"

• School activities

• Allies (family and friends) calling you

• Internet, TV and video games tugging at you

• Bright and shiny objects that distract you

• Other attractive people

• Any drama or soap opera in your life that takes your attention
• Anything that draws your focus away from your business
• Anything that gives immediate gratification and is more enjoyable than doing what you know you should be doing

The reason we come up with excuses is that we imagine the people we call are bigger, harder and scarier than they really are because the truth is that most of the people we deal with are very nice. The chances of true rejection are very, very small. But that isn't what we think in the moment.

In that moment of stress, when you have anxiety, your mind starts racing and thinking of others that you should be doing. Buddhists call this 'the monkey mind', where you have thoughts that lead to more thoughts that lead to anxiety that lead to fear, etc. Naturally, monkey mind contributes to call reluctance.

Since we're talking about how the mind plays this game, we also need to get real blunt about a truth you might not realize... and that is that people don't think about us as much as we think they do. People are usually so wrapped up in their own lives and to-do lists and the conversations going with the monkey mind in their head that they really aren't paying you much attention. The only thing that can really stop getting conversations that matter to your business - and your potential buyer's life in a new home - is to stop reaching out and trying to have those sales conversations.

While we're minding your mind, let's talk about the power of your subconscious mind further in the next chapter.

~~~~~

Key Takeaways:
- Call reluctance is the emotional hesitation that causes you to avoid: making contacts, asking for business, asking for referrals.
- Top earners have a minimum of 50 conversations, 15 face-to-face meetings, at least one event and meals with their customers each week. The key is consistency, without hesitation.
- Sales conversations is a numbers game because not everybody can reject you 100% of the time.
- Focusing on how to handle your call reluctance and increase your appointments is the number one thing you can do to positively impact your bottom-line in your business.

- Higher lead generation creates increased follow-through.
- To ride the wave of increased volume means building relationships over time with multiple touchpoints.
- The Sales Snob unconsciously thinks that sales is a bad thing, that doing sales is beneath them, and that social hierarchy and status are potentially more important than making a living through sales.
- The Sales Snob has to overcome their social conditioning and shift their attitude from 'sales is bad' to 'sales is helping people'.
- Performance anxiety individuals have four 'flavors': Danny / Debby Downers, Know It All's, BFFs and Control Freaks.
- Loan officers like being social so when they get no's, it goes against the grain of who they are as a person.
- Taming performance anxiety means removing the fear of potentially striking out and getting more time at bat.
- The chances of true rejection are very, very small. But that isn't what we think in the moment.
- Monkey Mind happens with anxiety and is characterized by having racing thoughts that lead to more thoughts that lead to anxiety that lead to fear, etc.
- People don't think about us as much as we think they do, they are too busy worrying about what you think of them.
- The only thing that can really stop getting conversations that matter to your business - and your potential buyer's

life in a new home - is to stop reaching out and trying to have those sales conversations.

FREE Support

Just one call really can change your life. If you're ready to ramp things up to where you know they can be, go to:

CrushingCallReluctance.com/Call

It's Your Turn Now!

Your Two Brains

This chapter is for your inner science nerd because we're going to talk about how your conscious and subconscious mind work together to create your results. Is it necessary to go this deep in a book about how to handle call reluctance – a sales training book? Probably not.

BUT here's the thing… when you understand that call reluctance is actually hard-wired into your biology, you understand the wiring which gives you the option to related to it differently. You don't need to be ashamed of call reluctance being part of your past (did you catch what just happened there?) because it's how the brain is wired. It's not like you're CHOOSING to make the phone heavier or bigger or more monstrous than it is – it's your biological system trying to protect you.

Our biology doesn't know that we don't have to go out and fight for our food anymore – but we do have to deal with social pressures and it is still wired to protect us. Earlier, we shared about how we humans have core beliefs about our relationships, acceptance and reputation. And we also talked about how the brain will pump opiates into the body to compensate for a trauma. Put these together and you can see that contacting people, networking, sales activities – all of these will trigger a biological response to compensate for potential pain. The net result of it is that it's a form of resistance, also known as call reluctance.

Dr. Daniel Kahneman wrote a book called Thinking Fast and Slow, where he breaks down the brain in terms of structure and function. We have all heard about the subconscious mind and the conscious mind, but the way he breaks it down is really helpful. Here's a quick diagram of how he explains brain structure.

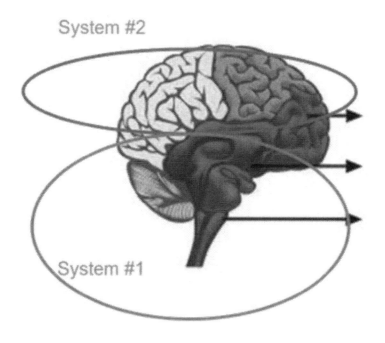

System Two is the prefrontal cortex, which was developed after System One, which is the primitive brain.

System Two, the prefrontal cortex, is the seat of our logic and higher thinking – the conscious mind. It's where our executive state is, our problem-solving, our language, our sales presentations and this is where we go to reach our goals.

System One is the earlier part of the brain, the more primitive part called the Mid-Brain, where the subconscious mind is located. It is one big system that runs on emotional states and is where hormones are managed. All really strong beliefs are held there because strong beliefs create habits that we automatically get through the day on by rote and, in this 'reptilian brain', those habitual behaviors correlate to a survival state. No higher thinking is needed – only response to unusual stimuli or emotions. It contains the fight or flight mechanism. And System One also uses our beliefs to make judgments on any given situation.

The number one thing to understand about System One is that it has one job – to protect and preserve your body and mind. While System Two is physically the larger part of the brain in terms of structure (the top 10% of the proverbial iceberg), System One is the hidden 90% of the iceberg where the real power lives.

Main Job of the System #1

Protect and Preserve the Body and Mind!

System One is vigilant in its job to protect your body and mind so it is constantly seeking information to make judgments (five times per second, it looks for input in everything around you).

So, if you're in a comfortable situation, System One lets you keep going with it while it's looking around your surroundings, and at what you're about to do, and what you're going to experience, and it's predicting what's going to happen. If it starts predicting, "Wait a minute, this goes against my beliefs," and remember that we all have those kinds of beliefs that drive us, System One will start making excuses to delay action and adjust your behavior while it continues to scan and assess the potential danger.

System Two requires attention, focus and for things to be orderly. It uses multiple muscles and logic skills.

Here is an example to demonstrate why that becomes important to know. Let's say you're driving a car down the road, and you're on the phone with me and I said, "*Hey, what's two plus two?*" Well, that's really so embedded in you that the response is found in System One. You say, "*Hey, that's four.*" No real effort needed to answer that question.

However, if you were asked a tougher mathematical question, you'd probably have to stop the car, pull over and think about it very logically. Your brain has a hard time multi-tasking and solving multiple problems at the same time.

And System One is very intuitive and wants to take the least amount of effort to get you what's needed, so it jumps to conclusions that are based on assumptions that use your beliefs to make judgments. It thinks in pictures and emotions. And it will make up stories if it has gaps in information, which is why people sometimes reach irrational conclusions.

At any rate, when you need to use logic to answer a question, it's going to ramp up and interrupt System Two to take the mental load of answering that complex question.

The Two Systems

System #1

- Intuitive and automatic
- Law of least effort; the easiest route
- The more it is use to an activity, the less mental energy it takes
- Risk loss adverse
- Avoids pain and goes for pleasure
- If there is a mental load, system #1 ramps up and interrupts system #2
- Beliefs are stored used to determine risk
- Jumps to conclusions and makes assumptions to fill gaps
- Creates a story to make sense of things

System #2

- Effort, attention, and focus is required
- Must follow rules
- Things must be orderly
- Deliberate
- Not good at handling multiple issues and problems
- While you're using it, your muscles tense up and your eyes dilate
- Logic, sales skills, language conscious problem solving
- It is hard to multi task here & solve multiple problems

System One is risk-averse for you because it's job is to protect your body and mind. It will do anything to keep you in the familiar because that is where it knows you are safe.

System Two is where your sales skills live because that's where your logic and language is located. System Two is also about problem-solving so it needs focus and order. It typically has a hard time multi-tasking for that reason.

Beyond that, when under stress, System One will start locking down and then System Two becomes taxed in response to that stress 'threat'. The result is that your brain will literally start to slow your judgment reaction times. For example, when in a public speaking environment, you might forget your speaking points. And your primitive brain, System One, will go to core belief issues – "*am I loved? Am I safe? Am I accepted? Am I going to survive here?*". This is literally what happens with call reluctance, which is perceived to be a potential threat to your well-being.

The chemicals of stress

Now, chemically what happens according to Dr. Nick Hall, who is a psychoneuroimmunologist (say that three times fast!) in Florida, is that different hormones activate in your system as a stress response. One is CRF, the corticotrophin-releasing factor, which starts to shut down higher brain function in System Two so you can focus on the core issue of getting back to safety.

Then cortisol starts kicking in at high stress levels, which gives you energy to get through the stressor (which creates the feeling of anxiety) and also boosts up your immune system. Why? Because something might happen to you – an injury or trauma – where you need to recover physically. That's why so many sales people and people under stress get sick, because there's so much cortisol being pumped through their system from being stressed that it actually wears down their immune system. Then, when they really need it to fight a bug, their immune system is depleted and they are susceptible to illness.

Epinephrine also speeds up your heart rate and gets your blood pressure up to pump blood to all the parts of your body. This is in preparation for the fight or flight response.

Then, lastly, norepinephrine kicks in your monkey mind. It starts running through all your beliefs to see how to solve the problem. And it will also leave a chemical marker on the hippocampus so that if you ever get in a tough situation again, your brain will remember it to avoid a similar situation in the future. It's really building to your belief system and saying, "*Oh yeah, let's never go back to here again, look at what happened.*"

The bottom line is that whenever System One perceives that failure, rejection or hurt may be coming, it will find something pleasurable and predictable to do. It will do everything it can to keep you rooted in the familiar. And that's the challenge.

The biology / behavior challenge

So, whenever loan officers are thinking, "I need to go make these calls", they don't know what's going to happen - their results are unpredictable. What message does that send to System One? "*Quick – go look at my notes from this morning, check my email, run to the office supply store, fix the printer, etc.*" – because those activities will yield a predictable experience.

On the surface, the thought makes sense – "*I need to take care of this first before I make my calls*" – because System One is skilled at feeding you what keeps you safe. But in the long run, it is jeopardizing your future in terms of revenues, results and lifestyle.

They've done studies where they hypnotized people to believe that a stapler weighs 7,000 pounds. Now, when under hypnosis and asked to pick up that stapler, that person cannot pick up the stapler! Researchers found that the hypnotized person, validated by electrodes connected to their brain and muscles, that the person will literally try with all their might to lift that stapler. They cannot pick up that stapler because they're under hypnosis, with the self-suggestion (or belief) that their biceps will try to pick it up but the subconscious mind gives signals to their other muscles, like triceps, that keep them from lifting it because of the suggestion that they cannot lift that stapler. That belief is preventing them from taking that action.

That's kind of what goes on in our mind. Your brain will go to the biggest picture you have and convince your system that it is not achievable or in our best interest to achieve it. And most salespeople never get trained on how to overcome this connection to separate our regular beliefs from what our beliefs need to be as salespeople. So we wrestle with it. It's like wearing a backpack with a ton of rocks in it while we're trying to climb our mountain – it just makes the job so hard.

Separating personal and professional beliefs

What we really need to do is disconnect our beliefs on acceptance in our personal lives and separate that from the beliefs about what we make it means in terms of acceptance in our career when we make calls as loan officers. It's literally a desensitization process.

In fact, it's just like the first time someone has a drink or a cigarette, when they probably think it tastes terrible but they keep doing it anyway. Your body and mind adjust and, after a while, it becomes habitual. The same thing happens when you focus on reducing the risk from call reluctance to make it more predictable and pleasurable. When you do that, the resistance to making calls tends to decrease and you find it easier to pick up that phone. It stops putting you in fear mode (of not being accepted and, therefore, banished to the wilds on your own) and you can make those calls without it being a matter of life and death.

The first thing to know about making this shift is that it's not a quick fix. Most of our students report that it's simple but not easy to make this transformation because they're going through a kind of 'valley of pain' to rewire their brain. It's about making a commitment and then sticking to it long enough to get through that initial dip in your resolve to make the change. It is natural to backslide after the initial excitement wears off – that's when the fear kicks in and it's when the average person will revert to old behavior. Keep going and you rewire your nervous system and your mind to handle and neutralize the no's; this is when call reluctance is no longer a factor for you.

Commit and Make Calls for 90 Days!

A lot of people can get this shift done in 30 days, some in 60 days, as you saw with our experiment with nine loan officers. For most people, though, it's good to allow 90 to 180 days to reduce the pressure and ensure that the new behaviors stick over time.

Secondly, once you're able to change your behavior and pick up the phone, our students report that it becomes habitual. The good news in that is that it's easier to pick up the phone for that third, fourth or fifth call to make the contacts and build the relationships. It has a compounding effect because these habits start building success with every phone call.

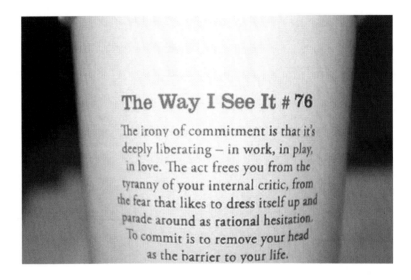

The Way I See It # 76

The irony of commitment is that it's deeply liberating – in work, in play, in love. The act frees you from the tyranny of your internal critic, from the fear that likes to dress itself up and parade around as rational hesitation. To commit is to remove your head as the barrier to your life.

"The irony of commitment is that it's deeply liberating in work, play and love. The act frees you from the tyranny of your internal critic, from the fear that likes to dress up and parade around as rational hesitation. To commit is to remove your head as to the barriers to your life."
~ Starbucks wisdom

Essentially, changing your relationship to call reluctance is a process of mental conditioning. The good news is that you can do a few exercises in just a few minutes a day, with the result being that the resistance to making calls will dissipate in short order.

Mental Conditioning

Five minutes a day

- Do the exercises that help you on a daily basis
- Then make the calls
- Your resistance will dissipate
- And you will think making contacts is as natural as calling a friend

 Interdiction:
Axe/Weaken The
Limiting Belief

 Redirect:
Rebuild A New Belief

Remember that there is an emotional belief that is creating call reluctance. That means logic is not going to be able to get at the belief, right? Instead, the antidote is action. Take the action by making the calls and, when you do that, the emotional belief gets re-wired with your new perspective and experience.

We'll talk about a few mental conditioning exercises you can do in the next chapter. But first, a quick word about change.

Change is the only constant

Change is the only constant. And it is everywhere because change is life renewing itself. And yet, change is the one thing we tend to resist, because our System One brain is trying to keep us safe by keeping us in the comfort zone of familiarity.

The good news is that you can bypass those System One warnings through mental conditioning and getting a fresh perspective on what you know and consider as comfortable. Once you understand what is happening, you can see the opportunity you have in defeating call reluctance to create the results you want in your business.

Next, let's talk about some mental conditioning exercises you can use right away to begin that shift.

~~~~~

Key Takeaways:

- When you understand that call reluctance is hard-wired into your biology, there is no need for shame or guilt when it shows up.

- Contacting people, networking, sales activities – all of these will trigger a biological response to compensate for potential pain.
- System Two was developed after System One – it is the prefrontal cortex and seat of higher reasoning – while System One is the primitive brain.
- System One has one job – to protect and preserve your body and mind. It is the hidden 90% of the iceberg where the real power lives. It is risk-averse. It is where fight-or-flight is activated.
- System Two requires attention, focus and for things to be orderly. It uses multiple muscles and logic skills. System Two is where your sales skills live because it's where your logic and language is located.
- When stressed, System One will start locking down and then System Two becomes taxed in response to that stress 'threat'. The result is that your brain will literally start to slow your judgment reaction times.
- Different hormones activate in your system as a stress response, which are linked to call reluctance.
- System One is skilled at feeding you what keeps you safe. But in the long run, it is jeopardizing your future in terms of revenues, results and lifestyle.
- You need to disconnect your beliefs on acceptance in your personal life from the beliefs about what you make it

mean in terms of acceptance in your career when you make calls as a loan officer. It's literally a desensitization process.

- It is necessary to experience the 'valley of pain' to rewire your brain by getting past the backslide to old behaviors as a reaction to the fear of the new.

- Changing your relationship to call reluctance is a process of mental conditioning.

Inquiry Form

Fill out this form, scan and email it to stay in touch, schedule a meeting with Carl and / or Kevin to discuss building your business faster and easier.

Your Name: _____

Business Name: _____

Mobile Phone: _____

Direct Email: _____

Website: _____

What do you want to discuss?

☐ **Call Reluctance:** You want personal strategies.

☐ **Business Systems**: Ways to streamline workflows and delegate for peak performance.

☐ **Team Development**: Talk about growing my team.

☐ **Business Coaching** with Carl and/or Kevin to grow my business.

☐ **Have Carl and/or Kevin Speak** at my next event.

☐ Other: _____

Please Email Your Image of This Completed Form to:
Carl.White@TheMarketingAnimals.com

13 Mental Conditioning Exercises

One way to disempower call reluctance is to honestly determine what the real odds of rejection are in a call scenario.

Exercise 1: Condition Your Brain!

To do this, commit to making calls for 90 days - no matter what. This simple act of commitment is very powerful. Eventually, your reluctance will dissipate and you'll think making contacts is as natural as calling a friend.

Be aware that the average person (which isn't you, right?) tends to fall back to old behaviors a couple of weeks into the process. It's natural but, at that point, you need to re-commit to the process to keep yourself from falling into the "Valley of Resistance and Pain."

Exercise 2: Determine: What Are the Real Odds of Rejection?

How many times in your life have you been rejected to the point that it deeply affected you and changed who you are as a person? For most people, the odds are that it happened only once or twice.

In other words, that kind of rejection is rare. So, in the mortgage business, how many times have you been rejected to the same extent? Normally, it never happens! The percentage is less than one percent that you'll be hurt deeply by calling clients. In other words, you have a 99% chance of success.

If you've been in sales for any amount of time, you have already faced rejection hundreds, or even thousands of times, and you're still standing. Bravo!

Exercise 3: Realize That You Are the Prize!

Make the mental shift and commit to realizing that you're the person helping others and are important to that outcome.

Here's an example of you can really help people: the average agent makes about 3% on a $200,000 house ($6,000). S/he does 8 buy sides a year. 8 X 2000 =

$16,000. That means every coffee appointment or lunch is worth $16,000. But what if you helped them get an additional, say, five closings in a year by simply closing their deals on time and now that satisfied buyer and seller refers their friends to these agents. That would be $30,000! So, through your actions, you're definitely helping the agents and their clients in a big way. Take the spotlight off of "you" and put it on "THEM"!

Exercise 4: Size Up the Real Fear and Bring the Bully Down to Size

Find a piece of paper and draw a pyramid on it or use a computer to generate one. Divide the pyramid into five levels. Then list the following fears.

At the peak is the fear, "They'll tell me No."

Below it is the fear: "Not knowing what to say."

Next is fear of the "Receptionist."

Below it is "Voicemail."

At the base, label the fear of "Dialing the phone."

Once you have the pyramid complete, go through the levels and cross each one off. For example, cross off "Voicemail" while you tell yourself, "Voicemail can't hurt me; it's only a machine."

Do the same for the other fears; cross them off one by one to get rid of them mentally. Essentially, you're convincing your cautious brain, System One, that you'll be successful and can handle anything that comes your way.

Exercise 5: Get an Accountability Partner

Having a partner or a coach or a team creates a feeling of acceptance. Preferably, find a partner who's already conquered call reluctance. Then, try the following team-building and acceptance tactics.

• Create contests to see who can schedule the most appointments.
• High-five and hug each other when you schedule an appointment.
• If you're in a small office, ask someone in another office to support and encourage you as you make phone calls.
• Use your virtual assistant as a monitor to make sure you make the calls, etc.

Exercise 6: For the Next 90 Days, Put Yourself into Situations in Which You Know You Will Get Rejected!

This is another way to desensitize yourself and realize that when people tell you "No," it doesn't matter. Try these fun methods of getting rejected every single day outside of the mortgage business:
• At a restaurant, come up with the craziest order.
• Test drive a dream car (Porsche, Lamborghini, Ferrari, etc.)
• Ask to fly a plane.
• Ask your utility company to lower rates.
• Ask your tax authority to lower taxes.
• Ask your credit card company to lower its rates.
• Ask your car lender to lower the rate, etc.

Exercise 7: Desensitize by Failing Fast!

For the next two to four weeks, double up and set a goal to make 100 contacts a week for 20 days. As a result, you'll make some progress, but you'll also become desensitized to the contact process.

By asking yourself, "*What could I do to improve?*" at the end of every day, you'll improve ten-fold. And, as a result, you'll get to the point where making 10 calls a day feels like no big deal – it's just what you do.

Exercise 8: Use Phone Burner

This is an automated system that will make calls for you and leave messages on voice mail. It relieves stress and saves a considerable amount of time. It works different than you may think and it comes with my highest recommendation and even partnered up with them. There's a 2 min video that you definitely want to watch which explains it and we have negotiated a discount for you at PhoneBurnerFreedom.com

Exercise 9: Use the Power of "No."

When you contact a client, use reverse psychology; that is, give them the power of "No" in your script. For example, say on the phone:

"I want to meet with you for 15 to 20 minutes. I want to discover what you're doing and share with you some unique things we're doing that may help you increase your sales volume. When we meet, I want you to feel comfortable any time during our conversation telling me if this isn't a good fit for you."

This lowers the wall of contact resistance while, at the same time, relieving stress on your part.

Exercise 10: Always Have a Second Offering

If you have a second, easier offering, then 63% of the time they'll say "Yes!" Most people are nice and don't want to feel like jerks. That means they often feel bad when they say "No." So, if you strike while the iron is hot, you may be able to get them to shift to and consider the less threatening offer.

Exercise 11: Turn Your Call to Action into Mental Problem Solving

You can turn your call to action into shared problem-solving by contacting a prospective referral partner and asking, "*What would it look like if we met for coffee and I could show you a couple of practical ways of increasing your income $30,000 to $50,000?*"

This kind of question shows your client immediately that you're interested in helping them reach the next level in their business.

Exercise 12: Track Your Numbers

People who track their results get better results. So analyze what you're doing. Use Excel spread sheets, forms, an online app or whatever system you like (email and texts do not count.) Be brutally honest; do not delude yourself.

You will likely be surprised at how low your numbers are initially. We humans tend to fool ourselves into thinking we're doing better than we actually are – so track those numbers and stay focused to be more productive and get more results.

Exercise 13: Use and Practice Scripts

Record your scripts and get used to your voice. Listen to each one 10 times and then say it out loud four or five times. This gets you used to saying the script, creating cellular memory, and it will become second-nature to you.

~~~~~

So, there you have it – thirteen ways to reduce or get rid of call reluctance. Our recommendation is to implement the exercises immediately! Choose one to start the ball rolling and then add others as you become more comfortable with them. And get ready to get more comfortable with... reduced stress and increased income. Call reluctance causes much less stress than does financial stress (I've had both).

Thor's Hammer

Yes, we are here to answer the burning question you never asked - you ARE related to a Norse god by virtue of your work as a loan officer! More on that in a minute...

So we've established that most sales people don't make enough calls and they don't do their follow-up calls. This one simple strategy is the game-changer. And we teach a system to make the most of it. (Remember the experiment with nine people who doubled their application volume? Get ready... you're about to learn how to throw the big hammer down!) – right after we cover the myths that might slow or stall your progress.

4 myths that block new results

We've talked about your two brains, and how your perceptions shape your experience and how it's important to focus your thoughts to get the results you want. Now, in all fairness, the thoughts you think are normal because they are your own. So you will need to be a little vigilant at the beginning about monitoring your mind.

Additionally, where you are today will be where you are tomorrow if you don't follow through on getting past the discomfort of new behaviors. It takes courage to step into a new commitment to yourself, your business and your customers. But you can do it when you don't buy in to the top four "reasons" (myths) that loan officers will often say about investing in these new behaviors.

1. Not having the time to live their best life.

When stepping up their prospecting by making more calls and scheduling more face-to-face meetings, some loan officers may feel that their time to enjoy life is being reduced. Yes, their time is being redirected but they need to remember that they will have the means to live their best life by following through on their commitment to make more calls, create more connections and cultivate more relationships.

2. Current circumstances predict the future so there's no point in trying.

Where you are now does not predict where you are going to be – that is pure B.S. (old, limiting Belief Systems – remember System One of your brain?).

Regardless of your circumstances, the only time to change them is now. It is never too late to make a change.

You may not be able to predict the future but you CAN predict that it will be different, based on the results we've shared with you, proven by our experiment with nine people and our years of industry experience.

3. <u>Going for the life you want is selfish.</u>

Author Ayn Rand wrote that it is both irrational and immoral to act against one's self-interest. Just as a car cannot run without fuel, you cannot give to others what you do not have... if you want to support others in living their best life, you must live your own best life. The path to doing so is to selfishly guard and invest your time in your business prospects and relationships. In 60 – 90 days, you will see the results of what being 'selfish' with your time (and taking time away from wasteful nonproductive activities that may have been done with the motivation of avoiding making phone calls) means today.

4. <u>That you have to be confident to live the life you really want.</u>

Fear always precedes achievement. The only time fear has a place is when someone is taking big, beaudacious action. Confidence (or lack of it) is simply a barometer of fear. As we've already said, the only antidote to fear is action; when you are in motion, your confidence naturally grows.

Oh – and it does not matter if you have tried and failed in the past. All that is relevant now is if you are willing to try again - this time using Thor's Hammer to get new results.

How to wield the big hammer

In the Freedom Club, we teach best practices to loan officers who follow the program by implementing specific tasks each day of the week.

This system begins every Monday with Thor's Hammer, where loan officers pound out 30 calls "pre-coffee" and "post-coffee".

Tuesday, there's a 'just ask' campaign to build their pipelines through 'who do you know?' with their current customers. As they update their current loans status, they ask their customers who they know as a potential referral using a very effective script.

Wednesday, these loan officers are calling their past database, which are often the easiest calls to make because they know these people, again, with a proven script.

Thursdays is the day for calling pre-approvals who are out looking for their new home and current agent partners to see who they are putting in their car to see properties that week. This may be the most effective "loan-getting" calls and scripts that we have ever seen.

(We can go over the specific scripts for each of those during your bonus strategy / scripting call that is your bonus for purchasing this book. Just go to CrushingCallReluctance.com/Call now.)

Fridays are a great day to catch up on everything else.

The goal of all this activity is that it all adds up to an average of around 53 calls a week and 10 – 15 face-to-face appointments. Another way to think of it is to have 13 personal conversations / day – not just phone calls – with 2 – 3 of those being face-to-face and then writing five thank you notes.

You want to make sure you text all your agents at least once a week and email all your other contacts once a week as well. It's all about simply giving the right messages and always including a Call to Action (CTA).

Here's a quick tip: since those people who know you are already friendly from either doing a deal in the past or you're working it with them right now, we call these types of calls stacking the deck. So let's stack the deck in your favor by calling people who are friendly to you, who know you and will jumpstart your calls with a smile. This can help you have a quick confidence boost because it's like calling your mother, or brother or a friend – because you ARE calling your friends.

Thor's Hammer will change you

When you are consistent about using this system, you will experience a kind of personal transformation. It might feel like all the air is getting sucked out of the room or you might feel like the air around you is a little swim-y or you might want to jump up and do a happy dance when you realize that who you are now is not who you were then in your business.

Real transformation – even when you're planning for – can sneak up on you and it changes everything. What you tolerated previously in your business won't be acceptable anymore. The attitudes that kept you playing small have no place in your life anymore. Basically, who you are now couldn't squish back into the little container of the old you anymore – because you have expanded and your business is reflecting that fact.

When you change your perceptions, beliefs and behaviors, everything has to change with you. Why? Because what's 'out there' is just a mirror of what's 'in here'.

From that place, when you think about call reluctance, you will find it's a non-factor. It can't hold you back anymore.

The real proof of this is in your results. Throughout this book, you'll find various tools to help you start creating a shift in your behaviors and beliefs. We recommend you take advantage of them to begin true training on handling your call reluctance. (And if you want more proof than what you're reading here, just call our office – we'd love to share more with you!)

~~~~~

Key Takeaways:

- Where you are today is where you will be tomorrow if you don't follow through on getting past the discomfort of new behaviors.
- You must be vigilant about how the four myths may show up to sabotage your new initiative.
- Fear always precedes achievement. Confidence (or lack of it) is simply a barometer of fear.

- Thor's Hammer is when loan officers pound out 30 calls pre-coffee and post-coffee.
- You can systematically increase your touchpoints.
- Stacking the deck means calling people who know you from either doing a deal in the past or you're working it with them right now.
- When you change your perceptions, beliefs and behaviors, everything has to change with you.

FREE Bonus

Let us help you crush call reluctance with some of our best tips and call scripts.

Why are we doing this? Because we want you to have your most awesome life and career.

And because we have your back.

Check It NOW at:

CrushingCallReluctance.com/Call

Summary and Next Steps

If you made it this far, you are ready to create different results by making more calls, helping more people and expanding your lifestyle. Choices can hold you back but chances can set you free. Take a chance on gaining new customers, new business and new freedom through picking up the phone backed by what you've just learned.

In business, there is a core truth – and a paradox – that you are in the process of working, and it is this:

Your business can only grow as fast as you do.

By you making the commitment to eliminating call reluctance, being willing to take new action and following through, you are showing up differently. You are growing yourself and, in direct proportion, you are likewise growing your business.

Cultivate your brain's ability to support you in having these new habits by being consistent. Don't confuse it by staying the course one day and then letting doubt, negativity or fear control your behaviors the next day. Instead, give it clear instructions by using the mental conditioning exercises and getting out of your own way by simply doing what you now have the tools to do better – picking up the phone, making new contacts and building your relationships. Your rewards for doing so will predictably show up in the next 60 – 90 days. Let THAT be your focus to keep your System One brain happy.

If this seems too good to be true for you, remember that "When the student is ready, the masters appear." That means you were ready to get new results in your business because that's what just happened here – you called in the resources and information you need to support you in eliminating call reluctance, changing your behavior and getting better results. So use Thor's Hammer and keep us posted on what happens for you and your business!

In closing, we encourage you to drop us a message and let us know what you've learned and how things are working for you in your business. Just visit the website at MortgageMarketingAnimals.com , listen to a podcast at LoanOfficerFreedom.com/ or attend one of our live training events, found at MasterMindRetreats.com to help you make a bigger difference with your buyers and agents through your business.

Carl and Kevin

P.S.: In case you need any more proof of the difference it will make in your life and business to handle call reluctance, pop back up to the Endorsements section to read what others like you have said about what happened when they crushed their call reluctance!

P.P.P.S.: If this brought up questions for you, please share them on our wall at:
Facebook.com/MortgageMarketingAnimals/ – we'd love to know! (Who knows? You may inspire our next book!) :+)

While you're at it, please make sure you visit us on Facebook.com/MortgageMarketingAnimals in any case and post a comment or a video about how much you what you just learned here in this book, ok?

The Freedom Club

The Most Powerful Group of Loan Officers in the World to Help You Get Better Clients, Close More Deals, Enhance Your Income

If you're a loan officer or Branch Manager closing 8 loans a month or more, then The Freedom Club is for you. As a member, you'll receive all the awesome benefits of Mortgage Marketing Animals.

In addition, you will have access to our full library of scripts for every occasion; loan checklists, systems and processes; job descriptions and ads; tracking sheets for leads, prospects, closings, and conversion rates; employee manuals; advanced loan-getting strategies and more.

Mastermind retreats every 90-120 days with other top-producing members are also included. Most importantly, you will receive personalized, one-on-one accountability coaching every two weeks. Here a plan will be designed specifically around you, your team, your market and your goals for the future.

Want a sneak peek at what it means to be in The Freedom Club? Check it out here:
CrushingCallReluctance.com/FreedomClub

If you have any questions, just give us a call at **(727) 787-2275.**

The "Get More Loans" MasterMind Retreat

Get the Latest Insider Strategies, Tips and Tools – And Have Fun At the Same Time!

Successful loan officers know that there is a big opportunity happening in the world of business right now. And it hinges on one key concept:

You have to know how to disrupt people's inertia, break through their comfort zones, get attention and share the right message at the right time.

What if you could get the insider information that helps you forecast market opportunities, gain the knowledge you need to prepare your business to take advantage of 'what's working now' and help support you with a great group of people who all want to see your success as much as their own – without spending weeks or months or even years to do it?

Introducing the Loan Officer MasterMind Retreat...

Learn more by watching this short video that describes the retreat experience at:

CrushingCallReluctance.com/3dayevent

Be A Guest on the Podcast

Twice a month, Carl brings you the best and brightest in personal interviews to discover the keys to success that are working in the field. This podcast is dedicated to inspiring loan officers to take the best of what they know to help them create the business results and lifestyle they really want.

Carl's style is casual, down-to-earth and practical. He empowers listeners while entertaining them and sharing tools, stories and strategies that can accelerate their mortgage loan business results.

Check out the podcast here:
LoanOfficerFreedom.com/

And if you would like to be considered for a guest spot on the show, just call our office at 727-787-2275 – we'd love to share your success strategies!

About Carl White

I am a husband, and a father to three wonderful young adults. My family and I enjoy boating, camping, and I am passionate about traveling the country on my Harley Davidson while masterminding with the  top thought leaders in the world.

On the business side of things, I am the Founder/ Chief Strategist of The Mortgage Marketing Animals and also the host of the #1 Podcast for loan officers in America.

I first began my venture into the mortgage business as a loan officer in October of 1999. Within eight months of opening the doors at Family First Mortgage, I became the top-producing branch out of approximately 336 branches nationwide. I also began to train fellow LO's in my "paint by numbers" approach. This technique helped the LO's retain more closings while working less hours in a week. Five years later, I opened up my own mortgage business called Time Mortgage.

Who I Help:
I help loan officers to implement proven marketing strategies that I have personally used in my own career, and had great success with, measured by hundreds of

thousands of dollars in revenue to me each and every MONTH. And while I make no income claims for you (of course), it is my belief that I may be able to help you increase yours.

How I Help:
I show specific step-by-step instructions on how to drastically increase your monthly loan production and income while working only 32 hours per week. I do this by teaching loan officers to hyper-focus their efforts, and to stop doing wasteful activities that they are currently doing that are not producing measurable results. By following the strategies that I provide, my clients are able to regain the freedom to do the things they want to do. Worrying about when and where the next deal will come from is no longer a concern.

Specialties:
Strategizing | Marketing | Advising | Speaking
Video Blogging | Marketing Seminars | Marketing Webinars
Generating Leads | Social Media Marketing | Video Marketing

Carl can be reached at:
Email: carl.white@TheMarketingAnimals.com
Phone: 727-787-2275
Website: MortgageMarketingAnimals.com/
Facebook: Facebook.com/MortgageMarketingAnimals
LinkedIn: LinkedIn.com/in/MarketingAnimals
Podcast: LoanOfficerFreedom.com/
Instagram: @themarketinganimals

About Kevin Gillespie

I'm happily married, with four children and 11 awesome grandchildren who call me Babu.

Janice and I enjoy traveling and learning about other cultures. Some of our favorite activities include curling (from when we lived in Wisconsin), wine tasting and driving our Jeep through the Texas Hill Country. I'm also enjoying learning how to play my guitar.

I've authored multiple industry articles, written and recorded a program for kids called Raise Your Grades and have just developed a program on overcoming call reluctance for Loan Officers.

My professional career path has led me to be a Branch Manager of Success Mortgage Partners, a business in Plymouth, Michigan. I now have more than 30 years of industry experience and have overseen $10+ billion in mortgage production.

I'm also a leader in the Mortgage Marketing Animals as well as Senior Partner/Developer of the Branch Academy, where we show branch managers how to develop and run a very profitable and rewarding business (instead of the branch running them).

I have other credentials and work history behind me but one of the things I'm most personally proud of is that my wife, Janice, and I were key in helping raise more than $1 million for the Wheel Chair Foundation. We've gone on mission trips to distribute wheelchairs for those who need mobility around the world, to places like China, Africa and Central America.

That was all made possible by my career, in what I consider to be the most honorable profession in the world – being a mortgage loan officer – helping buyers, agents and communities to live better lives.

Kevin can be reached at:
Email: Kevin@TheMarketingAnimals.com
Phone: 727-787-2275
Website: MortgageMarketingAnimals.com
Facebook: Facebook.com/MortgageMarketingAnimals

One Last Thing...

If you enjoyed this book or found it useful, we'd be very grateful if you'd post a short review on Amazon. Your support really does make a difference. We read all the reviews personally so we can get your feedback and make this book even better.

If you'd like to leave a review, then all you need to do is click the review link here:

CrushingCallReluctance.com/Review

Thanks again for your support!

Made in the USA
Columbia, SC
18 February 2022

56307686R00070